AMERICAN CIVIL WAR

Philip Katcher

Front cover illustration:
The battle flag, as used in the Army of Northern Virginia, marks this group as a typical group of field Confederate infantrymen, about 1862. Note that the officer (far left) wears the same uniform as his men, although he would generally wear something closer to regulation when off campaign.

Back cover illustrations:
Left: Noted historian Harry Roach wears a butternut version of a typical Confederate field uniform of the sort worn until 1863, when grey became a more common colour. Notice the variety of jacket buttons, and the wooden canteen. The stock of his P1853 Enfield has been decorated with a Union Army infantry cap badge, something which was actually done during the period and made the weapon easy to identify in a stack.

Right: Regulation trousers were sky blue and, indeed, trousers of this colour were often worn – whenever they could be captured from US Army supplies. This infantry sergeant wears a typical frame buckle and carries a blanket brought from home. His weapon is a P1853 Enfield rifled musket made, as were his shoes, in England.

1. Volunteers of the Charleston Zouave Cadets man the walls of Castle Pickney, overlooking Fort Sumter, near Charleston, in 1861, at the outbreak of war. The cadets, at present arms, wear grey uniforms with red cuffs, epaulettes, collars, caps and stripes on their trouser legs. The lieutenants wear the state regulation dark blue uniform. (National Archives).

CONFEDERATE FORCES OF THE AMERICAN CIVIL WAR

Philip Katcher

ARMS AND ARMOUR

2. A gathering of officers from South Carolina's artillery on Sullivan's Island, in Charleston Harbor, in early 1861 finds them all in the state dark blue uniforms. Captain A. J. Green, Columbia Flying Artillery, is the man standing on the left; the officer standing to his left wears the double-breasted coat of a field grade officer, while the rest are company-grade officers. (National Archives)

3. Virginia's leading military organization of 1861 was its 1st Infantry Regiment. In the foreground of this 1859 photograph are men from the regiment's Company A (Richmond Greys), while the man in the double-breasted coat is from its Company K (Virginia Rifles). The men wear overcoats for winter over their grey jackets. (National Archives)

INTRODUCTION

irst published in Great Britain in
'990 by Arms and Armour Press,
illiers House, 41-47 Strand,
ondon WC2N 5JE.

istributed in the USA by Sterling
ublishing Co. Inc., 387 Park
venue South, New York, NY
.0016-8810.

istributed in Australia by
apricorn Link (Australia) Pty. Ltd,
.O. Box 665, Lane Cove, New
outh Wales 2066. Australia.

ritish Library Cataloguing in
ublication Data
atcher, Philip, *1941–*
:onfederate forces of the
merican Civil War. – (Fotofax).
. Confederate States of America.
rmy. Army equipment &
niforms, history
Title II. Series
55.80973
SBN 0-85368-982-2

ine drawings by Bob Marrion.

esigned and edited by DAG
ublications Ltd. Designed by
avid Gibbons; edited by Roger
hesneau; layout by Cilla Eurich;
ypeset by Typesetters
Birmingham) Ltd. and Ronset
ypesetters Ltd.; camerawork by
'&E Reproductions, North
ambridge, Essex; printed and
ound in Great Britain by The
den Press, Oxford.

One by one the Southern States, fearing that politics in the rest of the country would eventually cost them their slaves, seceded from the country founded less than a century earlier. The Southern soldiers of 1861 were enthusiastic, on the whole, in their support of the new Confederate States of America that the rebellious States formed.

In a short time, however, superior Northern and Western resources began to tell. Weapons which should have been made entirely with iron or steel components had to be made with brass; so brass became rare, and things which should have been made of brass – finials on cartridge boxes and buttons on jackets – were made of wood and lead. There was insufficient leather, so soldiers wore shoes made with cotton tops and carried percussion caps in cotton cap pouches.

These shortages began to tell not just in weapons of war, but in the 'little things'. Photographic chemicals and equipment, for example, had come from the North and grew scarcer as the war went on. Therefore, most of our photographs of Confederate soldiers were either taken early in the war, when there were still abundant supplies, or are of popular generals whose portraits could be sold to the public or else were taken by Northern photographers and show dead or captured Confederate soldiers.

Our impression of the Confederate Army and Navy is not, as a result, exact. Yet the motley array of uniforms and equipment we see in surviving photographs agrees with the written records. Fanciful volunteer uniforms from 1861 were worn until they were rags. Thereafter, soldiers often preferred uniforms and equipment from home or captured from Union Army supplies to those the government issued. Foreign visitors were sometimes amazed by the lack of uniformity in the Confederate Army, but they were just as amazed by its fighting abilities.

This is not to say that the Army and Navy had no dress regulations – only that there were as often ignored as followed. Generally, however, it is safe to say that Army officers followed regulations in wearing double-breasted grey coats with branch-of-service coloured pointed cuffs and standing colours. The average enlisted man wore a single-breasted, waist-length, plain grey jacket and most preferred light-coloured broad-brimmed hats to the regulation cap, which was a copy of the French Army cap. Sky blue uniforms were usually seen if a Union Army camp had been successfully overrun; otherwise, grey or brown prevailed.

Navy uniforms were copied from those worn in the Royal Navy, with one major difference: they were grey for both officers and sailors. This colour was not always popular with the traditionally minded seaman, and blue was worn at sea in the form of jackets and caps despite regulations.

After four years of desperate fighting, the South was finally overcome. Its legacy has lasted through to today, in films, books and 'living history' events. I wish to thank those 'living history' enthusiasts whose photographs appear in this book, as well as those who actually supplied such photographs, for their help.

Philip Katcher

◀4

5▲

6▼

. Drum Major E. R. M. Pohle
f the 1st Virginia Infantry in
pril 1861. His grey coat is
rimmed with light blue and his
ompon is red, white and blue;
he two-piece belt buckle bears
he arms of the Commonwealth
f Virginia. His sash is red, his
rousers sky blue and his
paulettes fringed with brass
houlder scales. (National
rchives)

. Private J. K. Ewing, 4th
irginia Infantry, in 1861,
earing a civilian-type shirt and
'Sicilian' cap. This cap was
specially popular in Virginia in
861 and was copied from those
orn by Garibaldi's forces in
taly. Ewing's regiment became
art of the famed Stonewall
rigade. Ewing himself was
ppointed a Second Lieutenant
nd was killed at Gettysburg.
Herb Peck Jr collection)

. Volunteer units of the prewar
outh generally wore stock
attern badges on uniforms that
aried tremendously in detail
rom unit to unit. The shako, as
his volunteer of an unknown
nit wears, was a standard
niform item, as was his dark
lue or green coat, fringed
paulettes and two-piece waist
elt bearing a state coat-of-arms
nsignia. (Author's collection)

. Many Virginia volunteers of
861, such as this man, wore
heir civilian clothing to war
ith only a military-type cap to
how their combatant status.
he cap is dark blue or green, a
ommon colour among Virginia
olunteers, with a shiny black
eak and chinstrap, the latter
nade with a non-functional
uckle. (Author's collection)

. Rifle units were popular
mong volunteers. Most wore,
s this man does, the vertical
ugle cap badge, in this case
ith the regular US Army dress
ap. Coats were usually dark
reen, although blue coats were
ften worn instead. The three
ows of buttons were common
mong volunteers. (Richard
arlisle collection)

7▲ 8▼

▲9 ▼10

▼11

9. These volunteers, photographed on 10 May 1861, are members of the Clinch Rifles, which became Company A, 5th Georgia Infantry. Their shirts are civilian-pattern, but they wear their Company's dark green trousers with a gold stripe down each leg and dark green caps with a cap badge that featured a gilt wreath around the Roman letters 'CR'. (US Army Military History Institute)

10. The 5th Company of New Orleans' Washington Artillery served in the Western theatre of the war while the rest of the battalion served in the Army of Northern Virginia. These 5th Company men were photographed at Camp Lewis, near Carrolton, Louisiana, in their dark blue uniforms with red trim. The man standing has two red chevrons on each sleeve, indicating the rank of Corporal. (Library of Congress)

11. Not all prewar volunteers were elaborately uniformed. This man, who is rather elderly for active field service, wears a flannel overshirt which was common among volunteers of 1861. He holds a sword bayonet for his unusual weapon which includes the patchbox of the M1814 rifle, the barrelbands, barrel and hammer of the M1855 rifle, and the lockplate of the M1861 rifled musket. (Herb Peck Jr collection)

12. Because images in ambrotypes and tintypes, two of the most common period photographs, were reversed (i.e., the left side appears on the right), many men reversed the position of their equipment and wore their belts upside down so that the equipment would appear on the correct side – hence this Tennessee volunteer's upside-down US belt plate. The weapon is an M1841 Mississippi rifle. (Herb Peck Jr collection)

12▶

▲15

13. This Tennessee infantryman is armed with an M1816 smoothbore musket that has been converted from flintlock to percussion. The revolver in his belt is a Colt. The letters on his cap front apparently stand for Fayetteville Guard, which became Company G, 1st Tennessee Infantry. The regiment fought at the First Manassas, in the Peninsular Campaign and at Sharpsburg, Fredericksburg, Gettysburg, The Wilderness, Cold Harbor and Petersburg, and it surrendered at Appomattox. (Herb Peck Jr collection)

14. General Robert Edward Lee, here photographed towards the end of the war, became one of America's most famous soldiers as a result of his leadership as commander of the Army of Northern Virginia. He was a Colonel of Engineers in the US Army and when Virginia left the US he followed his state into the Confederacy. After the war he became President of Virginia's Washington College, dying there on 12 October 1870. (Library of Congress)

15. Lieutenant General A. P. Hill was a graduate of West Point (Class of 1847) who served in the Mexican-American War and entered Confederate service as Colonel of the 13th Virginia Infantry. After distinguished performances in Northern Virginia in 1862, he was named a Lieutenant General on 24 May 1863 and given command of the Third Corps of the Army of Northern Virginia. He was killed near Petersburg on 2 april 1865. (Library of Congress)

16. General Lee (seated) was photographed on the porch of his Richmond home after the Army of Northern Virginia's surrender.To the left is his son, Major General G. W. C. Lee, who commanded troops in the defence of Richmond, and to the right is the elder Lee's aide, Colonel Walter Taylor. Lee wears a grey frock coat and matching trousers, although he usually wore a short grey sack coat and blue trousers in the field. (Library of Congress)

16▶

▲17 ▼18

▲19 ▼20

21▲

22▲

17. Lieutenant General N. B. Forrest, an uneducated man, was a brilliant cavalry commander in the Western Theatre. His troops captured Murfreesboro, Tennessee, in early 1862 and Fort Pillow in April 1864. In late 1864 his successes at Brices Cross Roads and Tupelo caused Union troops to fear for their communications. His troops were finally overwhelmed by superior forces at Selma, Alabama, in April 1865. (Library of Congress)

18. Lieutenant General J. B. Hood, one of the South's poorer commanders, lost his army in foolish attacks on Franklin and Nashville in 1864. His coat buttons are in pairs, apparently indicating the rank of Brigadier General after the US Army regulations, although CS dress regulations did not spell out differences in general officer dress. His cuffs are piped buff rather than merely buff. (Library of Congress)

19. Major General J. E. B. Stuart's frock-coat lapels are here buttoned back; his standing collar and cuffs are regulation buff. Stuart led the cavalry of the Army of Northern Virginia gallantly, although he was rather too concerned about his own reputation to be outstanding general. He died in action at Yellow Tavern, near Richmond, on 11 May 1864. (Library of Congress)

20. Major General Joseph Wheeler commanded the cavalry of the Army of Mississippi. Wounded three times in action, he rejoined the US Army during the Spanish-American War and retired as a brigadier general in 1900. His buttons are arranged in threes, which would indicate the rank of Major General in the US Army. (Library of Congress)

21. Major General George Pickett is best known for commanding the division that made the unsuccessful assault on Union Army lines at Gettysburg on 3 July 1863. His dark blue trousers are regulation, but he has disobeyed dress regulations with his dark blue collar and cuffs, the latter, uniquely, trimmed with gold embroidery. (Library of Congress)

22. Major General Mansfield Lovell was in command during the unsuccessful defence of New Orleans; thereafter he commanded a corps at Shiloh but held no other field commands. The three stars and wreath of his rank have been sewn on his all-grey coat and his buttons, in threes, apparently indicate his rank. (Library of Congress)

▲23

▲24 ▼25 26▶

23. Major General Arnold Elzy appears, in this photograph, to wear the insignia of a colonel; indeed, he served as Colonel of the 1st Maryland Regiment until promoted to brigadier general after the First Manassas. However, the faint four lines of a general officer's Austrian knot appear on each sleeve. The narrow gold lace on his shoulder is designed to hold a fringed gold epaulette in place. (Library of Congress)

24. Major General Benjamin Huger, an ordnance officer in the US Army before the Civil War, was relieved of field command after an inept performance on 12 July 1862. Thereafter he served successfully as an inspector of artillery and ordnance, mainly in the Trans-Mississippi Department. (US Army Military History Institute)

25. Brigadier General B. F. Cheatham served as a brigade, division, and corps commander in every battle the Army of Tennessee fought. His buttons are arranged in pairs; the standing collar of his waistcoat, which is probably buff in accordance with regulations, is folded down. His collar insignia is strictly regulation. (Library of Congress)

26. Major General William Mahone, a corps commander in the Army of Northern Virginia, wears a type of short jacket which was popular with Confederate generals in the field as a comfortable riding habit. His grey or tan slouch hat, with its non-regulation badge, was also the most common field wear for all ranks. (National Archives)

◀27 ▲28 ▼29

30▲

27. P. G. T. Beaureguard, here in the all-dark-blue uniform of a colonel of engineers in the Louisiana Army, had been breveted twice for bravery as an engineer staff officer during the Mexican-American War. He was in command at the Siege of Fort Sumter and was second in command at the First Manassas and Shiloh. A personality conflict with Jefferson Davis resulted in his never getting the top command he possibly could have handled. (Author's collection)

28. James Kemper was photographed here as Colonel of the 7th Virginia Infantry, which he commanded from the First Manassas to the Peninsular Campaign. He was promoted to Brigadier General on 3 June 1862 and was wounded and captured in Pickett's Charge at Gettysburg. The laydown collar (as opposed to the regulation standing collar) was common among Confederate officers, as was the absence of any coat trim other than collar rank badges. (Library of Congress)

29. Colonel John Gregg commanded the 7th Texas Infantry Regiment from its formation until he was wounded at Chickamauga. After recovering he was promoted to command the Texas Brigade of the Army of Northern Virginia and was killed 7 October 1864. Greg's plain grey frock coat lacks collar insignia, a practice allowed in the field after 3 June 1862. (Herb Peck Jr collection)

30. The three white officers are surgeons, while the black man appears to be their servant. One wears the common field sack coat. Confederate surgeons often had to make do with replacement supplies, as medicines had come from outside the South before the war and the blockade hindered resupply, surgeons having to use home-made cotton or flax thread instead. (US Army Military History Institute)

▲31

▲32 ▼33 34▶

31. Major J. S. Mosby was one of the South's most noted partisan leaders. His troops, designated the 43rd Independent Virginia Cavalry Battalion, operated behind Union lines in northern Virginia, forcing the use of large numbers of Union troops to protect the area. Here he wears a sack coat with an Austrian knot on each sleeve and holds a light slouch hat. (Library of Congress)

32. Captain James Tucker, 9th Florida Infantry Regiment, holding a dark-coloured slouch hat. The 9th was formed in Virginia in June 1864, largely from the old 6th Florida Infantry Battalion. It served in the Army of Northern Virginia until its surrender on 9 April 1865; Tucker was one of fifteen officers in the unit at the time. (Fritz Kirsch)

33. First Lieutenant Charles Harper was said to have been the first man killed from Guilford County, North Carolina. His volunteer's uniform is dark blue, with US Army-style shoulder straps worn to indicate rank. His forage cap is decorated with gold lace according to Confederate dress regulations for his rank. (US Army Military History Institute)

34. It was definitely against regulations to wear US Army-style shoulder straps to indicate rank, according to the 21 March 1861 Richmond *Daily Dispatch*. Yet Second Lieutenant J. B. Washington (seen here on the left), an aide to confederate General J. E. Johnston, was captured on 31 May 1862 and photographed then in a grey jacket with yellow trim around the collar, down the front and around each pocket and US Army shoulder strap rank insignia. (Library of Congress)

▲35 ▼36

▲37 ▼38

39▲

40▲

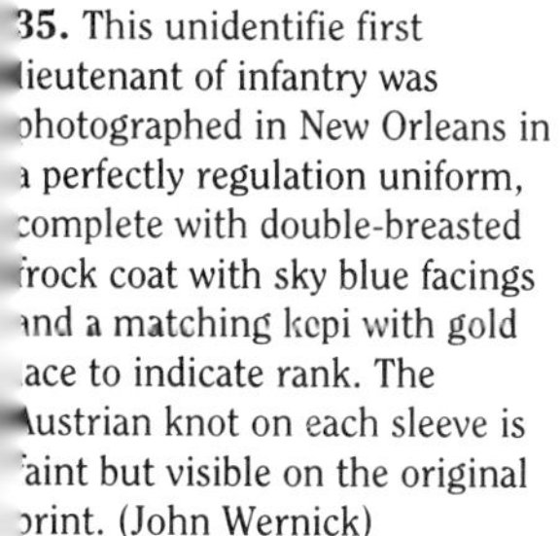

35. This unidentifie first lieutenant of infantry was photographed in New Orleans in a perfectly regulation uniform, complete with double-breasted frock coat with sky blue facings and a matching kepi with gold lace to indicate rank. The Austrian knot on each sleeve is faint but visible on the original print. (John Wernick)

36. First Lieutenant W. H. Young, an infantry officer from North Carolina, wears an unusually plain single-breasted jacket with gilt buttons and two gold bars on his collar to indicate rank. Each sleeve is marked with a gold Austrian knot, and his matching trousers have a dark stripe down each leg. His apparently dark blue cap is piped with light blue. (US Army Military History Institute)

37. This officer, apparently from Louisiana, wears a US Army belt plate with its silver wreath around a gilt eagle. His pistol holster is made with the pistol butt facing the rear; most had the butt facing the front. Most Confederate officers attempted to follow dress regulations. (John Wernick)

38. Enlisted men were rarely able to follow dress regulations by wearing double-breasted frock coats. Nevertheless, this non-commissioned officer has managed to obtain one, albeit without coloured collar or cuffs. The star over the chevrons should indicate the rank of Ordnance Sergeant, but similar stars were worn unofficially by large numbers of colour sergeants. (US Army Military History Institute)

39. While regulations offered no special insignia for company quartermaster sergeants, some followed the lead of the US Army in using the chevrons worn here by Company Quartermaster Sergeant Archibald Johnston, The British Guard. The Mobile, Alabama, unit was a local defence force that was captured on the city's fall in 1865. (Ernest Brown collection)

40. Sergeant Page Baker, Louisiana Guards, 1st Special Battalion, Louisiana Infantry, wears what appears to be a lieutenant's cap with his sergeant's jacket. The epaulettes, collar, cuffs and chevrons may be black or red; black was a common colour for sergeant's chevrons regardless of branch of service. Such trimmed jackets were rare after 1862. (US Army Military History Institute)

A: The British-made P1853 Enfield rifled musket, and its later variations, was the standard infantry longarm in the Confederate Army.

B: This copy of the British Army's knapsack was made by S. Isaacs, Campbell, in London for the Confederate Army. The company had been formed for the sole purpose of producing military supplies for the South. The knapsack was made of black rubberized canvas with leather corner reinforcing.

C: The Louisiana belt plate, as worn by the Louisiana Tigers and other Louisiana troops, featured a pelican feeding its young in a nest. The belt plate was a solid brass casting.

D: All the rifled muskets and carbines made by the London Armoury were produced for the Confederate Army. This is the lockplate of one of the company's rifled muskets.

E: This Confederate-made tin canteen is a copy of the US Army-issue canteen. It uses a carved wooden stopper instead of the US Army's cork stopper and its strap is a converted musket sling.

F: This novel drum-style, Southern-made canteen was produced by nailing together two shaped pieces of wood. The original is in the Confederate Museum in Richmond, Virginia.

G: Most Southern-made wooden canteens resembled small barrels. This one has a leather strap, but coarse cotton straps which could not be adjusted for different lengths were also used.

H: Wheat's Louisiana Tigers were recruited from among the Irish along the docks of New Orleans in 1861 and fought well at the First Manassas. After their commander was so badly wounded that he could no longer serve during the Peninsula campaign, the unit fell apart for lack of discipline. The jackets were dark blue with red trim; the fezzes were red with blue tassels; the trousers were blue and white striped (some say that they were made of bed ticking); and the gaiters were white.

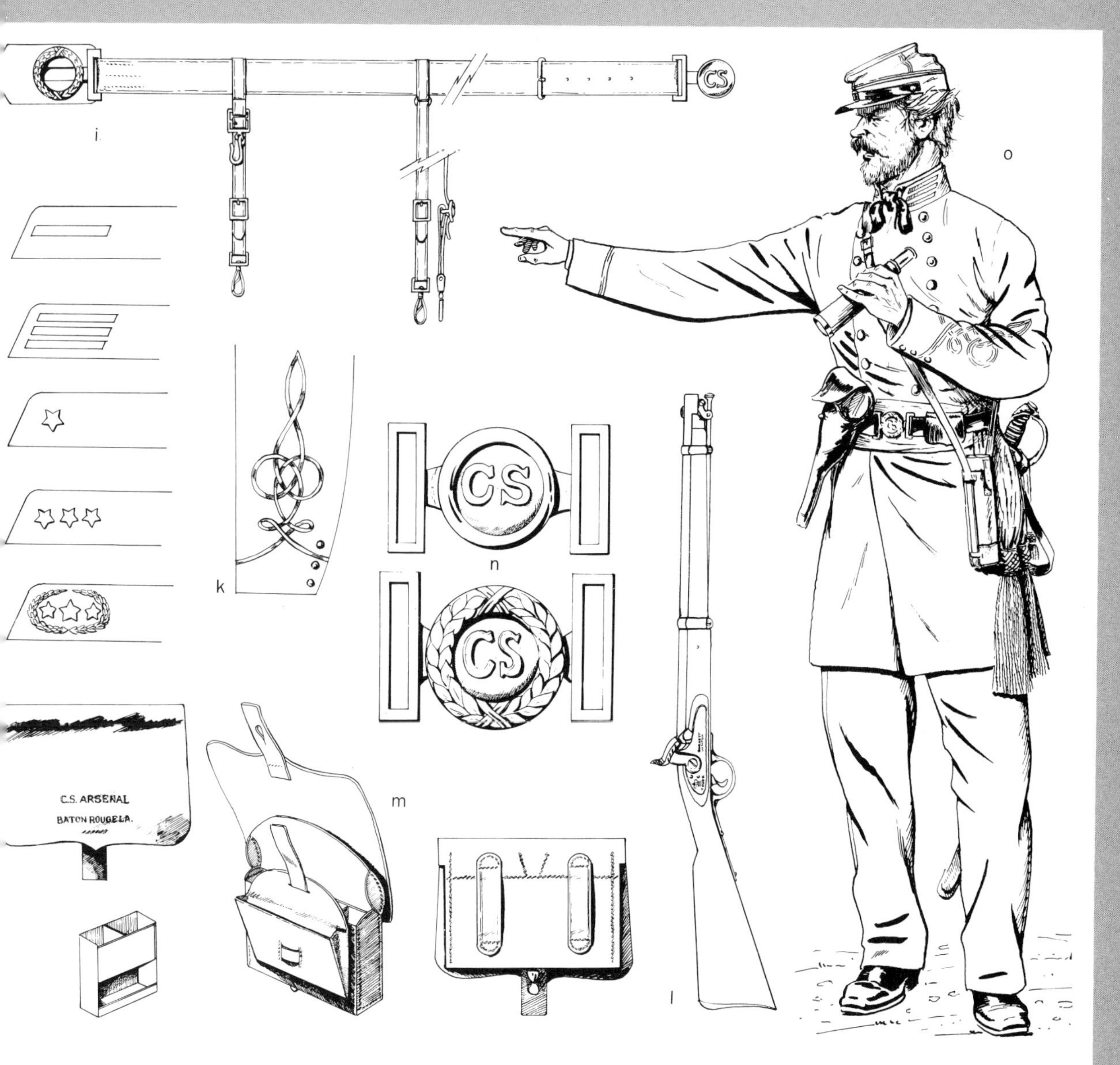

A typical example of an officer's sword belt. Examples in both sset brown and black leather are known, although black was e regulation colour. The two-piece belt plate was worn by ounted men as well as officers.

Officers' collar insignia were worn on branch of service loured collars. The ranks indicated are (from the top) Second eutenant, Captain, Major, Colonel and General. The same signia were worn by brigadier generals, major generals, utenant generals and generals.

The gold Austrian knot was worn on each officer's sleeve. The ngle braid here indicates a lieutenant; two knots, a captain; ree, a field-grade officer; and four, a general-grade officer.

The British-made P1858 cavalry carbine was the most mmon Confederate carbine. This particular example was ade by the London firm of Barnett.

M: This cartridge box for the 0.58-calibre rifled musket was made by the Confederate arsenal in Baton Rouge, Louisiana. It came with a single pair of loops, so that it could be carried on the waist belt, and an inner pouch for musket tools and patches. Two tin containers, as shown on the left, kept the ammunition safe.

N: The most common mounted man's and officer's belt plate bore the letters 'CS' within a wreath; the variation on top was less common but still worn, while a still rarer variation used the letters 'CSA' within the wreath.

O: The rank of this captain in regulation dress is indicated by the two stripes on the front, sides and back of his kepi; the three bars on his collar; and the two stripes in his Austrian knot on his sleeves. His sword is a foot officer's style, indicating that he is in the foot artillery or infantry.

CHRONOLOGY

Note: Some battles received different names from the opposing sides; for example, what the Confederates called Sharpsburg the Union forces called Antietam. Confederate names have been used in this list.

1860

6 November: Abraham Lincoln elected US President.
20 December: South Carolina votes to leave the US.
31 December: The US government refuses to abandon its property in South Carolina, despite state demands that it do so.

1861

9 January: Mississippi votes to leave the US.
10 January: Florida votes to leave the US.
11 January: Alabama votes to leave the US.
19 January: Georgia votes to leave the US.
26 January: Louisiana votes to leave the US.
1 February: Texas votes to leave the US.
7 February: The Choctaw Indian Nation votes to side with the South.
9 February: Jefferson Davis and Alexander Stephens elected President and Vice-President respectively of the Provincial Government of the Confederate States of America.
19 February: Confederate government formed in Montgomery, Alabama.
21 February: CS Navy authorized.
4 March: First national 'stars and bars' flag adopted.
6 March: CS Army authorized.
11 March: CS Constitution adopted.
16 March: CS Marine Corps authorized.
19 April: War Department orders Army uniform of dark blue smocks, steel grey trousers, forage caps and red or white shirts.
12–13 April: Siege of Fort Sumter, South Carolina (CS victory).
17 April: Virginia votes to leave the US.
6 May: Arkansas and Tennessee join the Confederacy.
20 May: North Carolina votes to leave the US.
21 May: Richmond, Virginia, is named capital of the CSA.
6 June: Final Army dress regulations published.
21 July: Battle of First Manassas (CS victory).
10 August: Battle of Wilson's Creek, Missouri (CS victory).
19 August: Missouri forms alliance with CSA.
22 October: Beginning of New Mexico invasion.
29 November: Missouri admitted into CSA.
9 December: Kentucky admitted into CSA.

1862

18 January: Confederate Territory of Arizona formed.
6–16 February: Forts Henry and Donelson fall (US victory).
21 February: Capture of Albuquerque and Sante Fe, New Mexico (CS victory).
22 February: CS government named Permanent and no longer Provisional.
6–8 March: Battle of Pea Ridge, Arkansas (US victory).
9 March: USS *Monitor* stands off CSS *Virginia* (US victory).
23 March: Battle of Kernstown, Virginia (US victory).
5 April–2 July: Peninsula campaign against Richmond (CS victory).
6–7 April: Battle of Shiloh, Tennessee (US victory).
7 April: Island Number 10 falls (US victory).
11 April: Fort Pulaski, Georgia, falls (US victory).
19 April: Army Signal Corps authorized.
29 April: New Orleans, Louisiana, falls (US victory).
1 June: Robert E. Lee given command of Army of Northern Virginia.
3 June: Army caps to be made with dark blue bands and rest in branch-of-service colours, with rank markings for officers; officers allowed to dispense with collar insignia in the field.
23 July: Regiments allowed to inscribe battle honours on colours.
29 July: Cruiser CSS *Alabama* launched at Birkenhead, England.
26–30 August: Battle of Second Manassas (CS victory).
14 September: Battle of South Mountain (standoff).
17 September: Battle of Sharpsburg (draw, but an effective US victory).
24 September: Great Seal of the Confederacy adopted.
8 October: Battle of Perryville (US victory).
20 November: Army of Tennessee organized.
13 December: Battle of Fredericksburg, Virginia (CS victory).
24 December: Fall of Galveston, Texas.
31 December–2 January: Battle of Murfreesboro (US victory).

1863

3 March: Day of national fasting and prayer.
23 March: CS Naval Academy founded.
1 May: Second national flag adopted.
1–3 May: Battle of Chancellorsville, Virginia (CS victory).
10 May: Major General T. J. ('Stonewall') Jackson dies.
16 May: Battle of Champion's Hill, Mississippi (US victory).
19 May–4 July: Siege of Vicksburg, Mississippi (US victory).
27 May–9 July: Siege of Port Hudson, Louisiana (US victory).
9 June: Battle of Brandy Station, Virginia (draw).
19 June: Volunteer CSN officers to wear gilt letters 'VN' on cap fronts.
1–3 July: Battle of Gettysburg (US victory).
17 July: Battle of Honey Springs, Indian Territory (US victory).
11 August: Large pro-US meeting held in Washington, North Carolina.
19–20 September: Battle of Chickamauga (CS victory).
25 November: Battle of Missionary Ridge, Tennessee (US victory).
26–28 November: Mine Run Campaign (CS victory).

1864

17 February: Army Invalid Corps authorized.
20 February: Battle of Olustee, Florida (CS victory).
27 February: Prisoner-of-war camp opened at Andersonville, Georgia.
5 May: Wilderness campaign begins; fighting in Virginia will not end until Lee surrenders.
11 May: J. E. B. Stuart mortally wounded.
13 May: Battle of Resaca; first major battle in Atlanta campaign.
10 June: Battle of Brice's Crossroads, Mississippi (CS victory). Congress authorizes drafting of men aged 17 to 50.
19 June: CSS *Alabama* sunk off French coast.
2–14 July: Early's Raid against Washington, DC (US victory).
20 July: Battle of Winchester, Virginia (US victory).
22 July: Battle of Atlanta, Georgia (US victory).
5 August: Battle of Mobile Bay, Alabama (US victory).
1 September: Atlanta abandoned.
8 October: Cruiser CSS *Shenandoah* sails from England.

15 November–10 December: Sherman's troops march from Atlanta to Savannah on the Atlantic coast.
25 November: Plot to burn New York City fails.
20 December: Savannah abandoned.

1865
15 January: Fort Fisher, North Carolina (last Southern port open) falls.
6 February: Robert E. Lee named General-in-Chief of the Armies of the Confederate States.
18 February: Charleston, South Carolina, falls.
2 March: Lee writes to Grant proposing meeting to discuss peace negotiations; offer is refused.
4 March: Last national flag adopted.
6 March: Battle of Natural Bridge, Florida (CS victory).
13 March: Blacks authorized to serve in the Army.
18 March: CS Congress adjourns for last time.
19–21 March: Battle of Bentonville, North Carolina (last major battle of the war: US victory).
1 April: Battle of Five Forks, Virginia (US victory).
3 April: Richmond, Virginia, falls.
9 April: Army of Northern Virginia surrenders to Army of the Potomac.
12 April: Mobile, Alabama (last major Southern city in Confederate hands) falls.
26 April: General Joseph Johnston's army surrenders in North Carolina.
26 May: Trans-Mississippi command surrenders.
6 November: CSS *Shenandoah* surrenders to British authorities.

ARMIES AND CORPS OF THE CONFEDERACY

Army of the Shenandoah: Formed near Harper's Ferry, Virginia, 21 April 1861. Merged into the Army of the Potomac July 1861. Commanders: Maj. Gen. K. Harper; Col. T. J. Jackson; Brig. Gen. J. E. Johnston.
Army of the Peninsula: Formed 26 May 1861. Merged into the Army of Potomac 12 April 1862. Commander: Col. J. B. Magruder.
Army of the Northwest: Formed in Western Virginia 8 June 1861 and dissolved 9 February 1862. Commanders: Brig. Gens. R. S. Garnett and H. R. Jackson; Maj. Gens. W. W. Loring, E. Johnson.
Army of the Potomac: Formed 24 May 1861 in Northern Virginia; merged into Army of Northern Virginia 1 June 1862. Commanders: Gens. P. G. T. Beaureguard, J. E. Johnston.
Army of Northern Virginia: Formed 1 June 1862; surrendered 9 April 1865. Commander: Gen. Robert E. Lee.
I Corps: Formed 6 November 1862. Commanders: Lt. Gen. J. Longstreet; Maj. Gen. R. H. Anderson.
II Corps: Formed 6 November 1862. Commanders: Lt. Gens. T. J. Jackson, R. S. Ewell, J. A. Early, J. B. Gordon.
III Corps: Formed 30 May 1863. Commander: Lt. Gen. A. P. Hill.
IV Corps: Formed 19 October 1864. Commander: Lt. Gen. R. H. Anderson.
Cavalry Corps: Formed 30 May 1863. Commanders: Maj. Gens. J. E. B. Stuart, Fitzhugh Lee; Lt. Gen. Wade Hampton.
Army of the Kanawha: Formed 11 August 1861 in Western Virginia; dissolved early 1862. Commander: Brig. Gen. J. B. Floyd.
Army of Eastern Kentucky: Formed from local militia 1861; dissolved 1862. Commander: Brig. Gen. H. Marshall.
Army of New Mexico: Formed in Texas 14 December 1861; dissolved in December 1862. Commander: Brig. Gen. H. H. Sibley.
Army of Louisiana: Formed from Louisiana State troops 1861 and dissolved shortly afterwards. Commander: Brig. Gen. P. O. Hebert.
Army of Pensacola: Formed near Pensacola, Florida, 22 October 1861; dissolved after that town's evacuation 9 May 1862. Commander: Brig. Gen. A. H. Gladden.
Army of Mobile: Formed near Mobile, Alabama, 27 January 1862; dissolved 27 June 1862. Commander: Maj. Gen. J. M. Withers.
Central Army of Kentucky: Formed in Kentucky September 1861; merged into Army of the Mississippi 29 March 1862. Commanders: Lt. Gens. S. B. Buckner, A. S. Johnston.
Army of East Tennessee/Kentucky: Formed February 1862 near Knoxville; redesignated Army of Kentucky 25 August 1862; merged into Army of Tennessee as Smith's Corps 20 November 1862. Commander: Gen. E. K. Smith.
Army of the Mississippi/Tennessee: Formed in Western Department 5 March 1862; became Army of Tennessee 7 November 1862; surrendered 26 April 1865. Commanders: Gens. A. S. Johnston, P. G. T. Beaureguard, B. Bragg, J. E. Johnston, J. B. Hood; Maj. Gens. W. J. Hardee, L. Polk.
I Corps: Formed 5 March 1862. Commanders: Maj. Gens. L. Polk, W. J. Hardee, B. F. Cheatham.
II Corps: Formed 5 March 1862. Commanders: Maj. Gens. B. Bragg, S. Jones, W. J. Hardee, J. C. Breckinridge, D. H. Hill, S. D. Lee.
III Corps: Never an official unit, it existed as a tactical formation. Commanders: Maj. Gens. W. J. Hardee, L. Polk, A. P. Stewart, E. D. Walthall.
Cavalry Corps: Formed 22 January 1863. Commander: Maj. Gen. W. J. Wheeler.
Army of Middle Tennessee: Formed 28 October 1862; merged into Army of Tennessee. Commander: Maj. Gen. J. C. Breckinridge.
Army of the West: Formed 29 Janaury 1862; later merged into Army of West Tennessee. Commanders: Maj. Gens. E. Van Dorn, J. P. McCowan.
Army of West Tennessee/Mississippi: Formed 20 June 1862; surrendered 4 July 1863. Commander: Lt. Gen. J. C. Pemberton.
Southern Army/Trans-Mississippi Army: Formed in West Lousiana and Texas 14 January 1863; surrendered 26 May 1865. Commanders: Lt. Gens. T. H. Holmes, R. Taylor.
Army of Missouri: Formed August 1864; later merged into Trans-Mississippi Army. Commander: Maj. Gen. S. Price.
Army of Mississippi: Formed December 1863 in Alabama, Mississippi, and East Louisiana; merged into Army of Tennessee 26 July 1864. Commanders: Lt. Gen. A. P. Stewart; Maj. Gen. E. C. Walthall.

UNIFORMS OF THE CONFEDERATE FORCES

Army and Marine Corps Commissioned Officers' Insignia

Gold embroidery worn on the front part of the coat collar:
General Officers: A wreath enclosing three stars, the centre one 1¼in and the others ¾in in diameter.
Colonel: Three stars arranged horizontally.

Lieutenant Colonel: Two stars arranged horizontally.
Major (Surgeon): One star.
Captain (Assistant Surgeon): Three horizontal ½in bars.
First Lieutenant: Two horizontal ½in bars.
Second Lieutenant: One horizontal ½in bar.

Gold braid worn on each coat sleeve in the form of an Austrian knot and on the top, sides, back and front of the cap:
General Officers: Four braids.
Field Grade Officers: Three braids.
Captains (Assistant Surgeons): Two braids.
Lieutenants: One braid.

Branch of Service Colours

Worn by all ranks on coat collars and cuffs and caps and as stripes on trousers by regimental officers and sergeants:
Infantry: Sky blue.
Artillery: Red.
Cavalry: Yellow.
General Officers, Staff, Engineers: Buff (dark blue caps).
Medical Department: Black.
Marines: Dark blue.

Sashes

Worn by officers and sergeants:
General Officers: Buff.
Staff, Engineers, Artillery, Infantry, Marine Corps: Red.
Cavalry: Yellow.
Medical Department: Green.

Army and Marine Corps Enlisted Sleeve Insignia

Chevrons worn above the elbow in branch of service colours for Army, points down, and in black, points up, for Marines:
Sergeant Major: Three bars and an arc.
Quartermaster Sergeant: Three bars and a tie.
Ordnance Sergeant: Three bars and a star.
First (Orderly) Sergeant: Three bars and a lozenge.
Sergeant: Three bars in worsted.
Hospital Steward (Army only; unofficial): Three bars and a lozenge in black.

Army Cap Badges

No cap badges were known to have been adopted officially, yet some were known to have been worn:
Surgeon: Old English letters 'MS', often within a wreath.
Ambulance Corpsman: Red cloth badge.
Signal Corps: White metal crossed signal flags.

Army Trouser Stripes

Worn on the outside leg of sky blue trousers for regimental officers and other ranks and dark blue trousers for other officers:
General officers: Two ⅝in gold stripes, ⅛in apart.
Staff, Engineers: One 1¼in gold stripe.
Surgeons: A 1¼in black velvet stripe edged with gold.
Regimental Officers: A 1¼in branch-of-service coloured stripe.
Sergeants: As for regimental officers.

CONFEDERATE NAVY DRESS REGULATIONS

Navy Relative Rank

There were two types of Navy officers, executive (deck) and civil. Each type had a unique title, but they all wore basically the same uniform, with differences indicated by the colour of the gold-edged shoulder straps and the 'executive loop' worn on the upper bar of executive officer cuff lace:
Admiral: Only an executive officer rank.
Flag officer: Only an executive officer rank.
Captain: Only an executive officer rank.
Commander: Surgeon, Paymaster, Chief Engineer or Naval Constructor over 12 years.
Lieutenant Commanding: Only an executive officer rank.
First Lieutenant: Surgeon, Paymaster, Chief Engineer or Naval Constructor under 12 years.
Second Lieutenant: Only an executive officer rank.
Master: Passed Assistant Surgeon, First Assistant Engineer.
Passed Midshipman: Assistant Surgeon or Paymaster, Second or Third Assistant Engineer.
Midshipman: Only an executive officer rank.

Naval Officer Branch of Service Colours

Each Navy officer wore a rectangular shoulder strap 4½in long and 1⅜in wide on each shoulder, edged with gold embroidery and bearing his rank insignia in gold within, on a ground of a different colour according to branch of service:
Executive Officers: Sky blue.
Medical Officers: Black.
Paymasters: Dark Green.
Engineers: Dark blue.
Naval Constructors: Buff.

Naval Officer Shoulder Strap Insignia

Admiral:* Five stars.
Flag Officer: Four stars.
Captain: Three stars.
Commander: Two stars.
Lieutenant commanding:* Two stars.
First Lieutenant:* One star.
Second Lieutenant:* Plain.
Master: Plain.
Passed Midshipman: A gold strip 4in long and ½in wide.
Civil officers over 12 years: Two crossed olive or live oak sprigs.**
Civil officers under 12 years: One olive or live oak sprig.**
Civil officers ranked with masters: Two olive leaves.***
Civil officers ranked with Passed Midshipmen: Plain***
*After 1862. **Olive worn by surgeons and paymasters, live oak by engineers and naval constructors. ***No insignia given for engineers.

Naval Officers' Cuff Lace Insignia

Bars of ½in-wide gold lace worn around each cuff to indicate rank. The top bar was looped, after the style worn by officers of the Royal Navy but ending in more of a point, with lace worn by executive officers.

	1861	1862
Admiral*	–	Five
Flag Officer	Four	Four
Captain	Three	Three
Commander	Two	Two
Lieutenants Commanding*	Two	Two
Lieutenant	One	One**
Second Lieutenant*	–	One
Master	One***	One
Passed Midshipman	3 large buttons	3 large buttons
Midshipman	3 medium buttons	3 medium buttons

*Rank created in 1862. **Redesignated First Lieutenant in 1862. ***Lace was ¼in wide.

Naval Officer Cap Badges

Admiral: Gold wreath, fouled anchor, five stars.
Flag Officer: As above with four stars.
Captain: As above with three stars.
Commander: As above with two stars.
Lieutenant Commanding: As above with two stars.
First Lieutenant: As above with one star.
Second Lieutenant: As above with no stars.
Master: As above with no stars.
Passed Midshipman: Plain fouled anchor.
Civil officer over 12 years: Gold wreath and three stars.*
Civil officer under 12 years: As above with two stars.*
Civil officer rating as Lieutenant: As above with one star.
Civil officer rating below Lieutenant: As above with no stars.
*Engineers also wore the letter 'E' and Naval Construtors the letter 'C' under the stars within the wreath.

THE CONFEDERATE ARMED FORCES IN STATISTICS

Combat Units of the Confederate Army

Unit	Number
Cavalry Regiments	137
Cavalry Battalions*	143
Cavalry Legions**	1
Independent Cavalry Companies	101
Artillery Regiments	16
Artillery Battalions	25
Independent Artillery Companies	227
Infantry Regiments	642
Infantry Battalions	163
Infantry Legions	9
Independent Infantry Companies	62

*A battalion had two fewer companies than a regiment – a practice dating from the eighteenth century when the two regimental flank companies, one of grenadiers and the other of light infantry, were removed, to leave the battalion as a main combat unit. **A legion was a combined-arms force including cavalry, artillery and infantry in different proportions.

Strength of the Confederate Army

Estimated total enlistments
1,227,890 to 1,406,678

Losses in the Confederate Army

Note: Because of the destruction of many official documents on the war's end, figures are not exact, but estimated.

Killed	52,954*
Died of wounds	21,570
Died of disease	59,297

*Excludes Alabama figures; better total estimate is some 94,000.

Top Ten Fighting Regiments
(as indicated by battle losses)

Regiment	*Battle*	*Losses (%)*
1st Texas	Sharpsburg	82.3
21st Georgia	Manassas	76.0
26th North Carolina	Gettysburg	71.7
6th Mississippi	Shiloh	70.5
8th Tennessee	Stone's River	68.2
10th Tennessee	Chickamauga	68.0
Palmetto Sharpshooters	Glendale	67.7
17th South Carolina	Manassas	66.9
23rd South Carolina	Manassas	66.2
44th Georgia	Mechanicsville	65.1

THE CONFEDERATE NAVY (AUGUST 1862)

Wooden converted war vessels	44
Navy-built wooden war vessels	12
Partially-built vessels	9
Navy-built iron-clad war vessels	12
Vessels being built currently	23

Strengths of the Confederate Navy

	Officers	*Ratings*
1861	79	Unknown
1864	753	3,674

Strengths of the Confederate Marine Corps

Year	*Total* (officers and men)
1861	350
1862	560
1864	539

WEAPONS OF THE CONFEDERATE ARMY

Note: Quoted material and numbers are taken from the Ordnance Field Manual, published by the Confederate Army in Richmond in 1862.

FIELD ARTILLERY

Gun Howitzer, Bronze (Napoleon): Smoothbore. Tube bronze; weight 788lb; length 58.6in; range (at 3° 45′ elevation) 1,300yd. Firing a 12lb shot, this was the preferred Confederate field artillery piece.

Gun Howitzer, Iron (1862 field model): Smoothbore. Tube iron; weight 850lb; length 64.4in; range (at 3° 30′ elevation) 1,200yd. An adaptation of the Napoleon which used iron instead of the scarcer bronze.

10-pound Parrott: Rifled. Tube iron; length 72.8in; range (at 6°) 1,950yd. Similar to the 3in rifle save for a band around the breech, this US Army weapon was highly accurate at long range. Some 3in rifles were converted into Parrott guns by having an iron band applied at the breech at Richmond's Tredegar works.

3-inch rifle (M1861): Rifled. Tube iron; weight 967lb; length 67in; range (at 6°) 2,250yd. Firing a 10lb shot, this weapon was especially accurate at long range and good for counter-battery work.

INFANTRY LONGARMS

M1841 Rifle (Mississippi): Rifled; 0.54-calibre. Length 52.66in; barrel length

33in. Browned barrel and lock; brass mountings. A common early war weapon, taking a sabre bayonet.
M1842 Musket: Smoothbore; 0.69-calibre. Length 57.75in; barrel length 42in. Bright-finished iron furniture. Although obsolete, this weapon was often issued, especially in the early years of the war.
M1855 Rifled Musket: Rifled; 0.58-calibre. Length 74in; barrel length 40in. Bright-finished iron furniture. The Richmond Armory produced 11,762 copies of this US Army weapon.
M1855 Rifle: Rifled; 0.55-calibre. Length 72in; barrel length 33in. Iron barrel and lock; brass mountings. The Fayetteville Armory, North Carolina, made some 20,000 copies of this US Army weapon.
P1853 Rifled Musket (Enfield): Rifled; 0.577-calibre. Length 55in; barrel length 39in. Bright-finished iron barrel and lock; brass mountings. The regulation British Army longarm of the period. The Confederates imported some 115,000 of these weapons from Britain as well as making perhaps 20,000 copies in the South.
M1854 Lorenz Rifled Musket: Rifled; 0.54-calibre. Length 52.7in. Bright iron finish. The regulation Austrian Army weapon of the period. The Confederates imported about 100,000 of this somewhat crude weapon.

CARBINES
M1855: Rifled; muzzle-loading; 0.58-calibre. Length 41.5in. Bright iron finish. A cut-down version of the Richmond Armory's M1855 rifled musket. Some 19,764 were made until the machinery for manufacturing the weapons was shipped to Tallahassee, Alabama, in mid-1864.
P1856 Carbine (Enfield): Muzzle-loading; 0.577-calibre. Length 37in. Iron lock and barrel; brass mountings. This British Army weapon was both widely imported and manufactured in the South. It was eventually named as the regulation cavalry carbine, and the Government's Tallahassee Armory in Alabama produced some 900 examples by the end of the war.
M1859 Sharps: Rifled; breech-loading; 0.52-calibre. Length 37.75in. Polished iron metal parts. The basic method of obtaining these highly sought-after weapons was by capture from the US Army. However, a private factory, later taken over by the Government, was set up in Richmond and eventually made some 5,200 copies of this weapon.

REVOLVERS
M1860 Colt Army: 0.44-calibre. Length 14in. A US Army weapon, but prewar supplies and wartime captures allowed this to be a standard cavalry hand gun.
M1851 Colt Navy: 0.36-calibre. Length 13in. Some 15,800 Southern-made copies of this US Army hand gun were produced. With large numbers in the South before the war and the capture of quantities of the weapon during the war, this became the standard Confederate cavalryman's and officer's hand gun. Southern-made versions often replaced the iron frames with brass and eliminated the cap guards behind the cylinders.
Grape-shot Pistol: 0.40-calibre (9 rounds); 16-gauge (one round). Barrel length 7in. An odd weapon with a cylinder revolving around another barrel which fired a load of buckshot, the LeMat was invented by a dentist from New Orleans and was produced for the Confederate Army and Navy in Britain and France. Some 2,500 were made.

EDGED WEAPONS
Cavalry Sabre: Length 43.25in; brass hilt with leather-wrapped wooden grips; blade width 1.1in in the middle; metal scabbard. Officially, 'Curved blade 36 inches long, hilt guard and scabbard of sheet steel'. These weapons were usually crude copies of the US M1840 o M1861 cavalry sabres, with reddish brass hilts.
Mounted Artillery Sabre: Length 38.6in; single brass guard and leather-wrapped grips; blade width 1.06in in the middle; metal scabbard. Officially, 'This differs from the cavalry sabre in having a blade only 32 inches long, though of greater curvature. It also has a hilt, guard and scabbard'. Again copies of the US M1840 light artillery sabre, few of these weapons were made or issued.
Foot Artillery Sword: Length 26in; all-brass hilt; blade width 1.8in in the middle; leather scabbard. Officially, 'Has a straight two-edged blade 19 inches long, narrower near the hilt than in the middle, a hilt and leather scabbard'. A copy of the US Army M1833 foot artillery sword and a weapon virtually never seen in use.
Infantry Sword: Length 38.75in; all-brass hilt; blade width 0.72in in the middle; leather scabbard. Officially, 'Has a blade straight (cut and thrust) 32 inches in length, a hilt, guard and leather scabbard. This sword is for the non-commissioned officers of foot troops. The sword for officers not mounted is of the same pattern, with ornamented mountings'. The NCO sword was rarely seen, and most officers used copies of the US Army M1850 line officer's sword with its slightly curved blade rather than the straight blade of the NCO's sword.

41. Early-war uniforms were often elaborately trimmed, usually in black or red. This corporal's jacket has false epaulettes made simply by sewing lace in epaulette form or each shoulder. His unit is unknown. The same trim is used around the cuffs and collar and jacket edges as well as on each trouser leg. (Author's collection)

42▲

43▲ 44▼

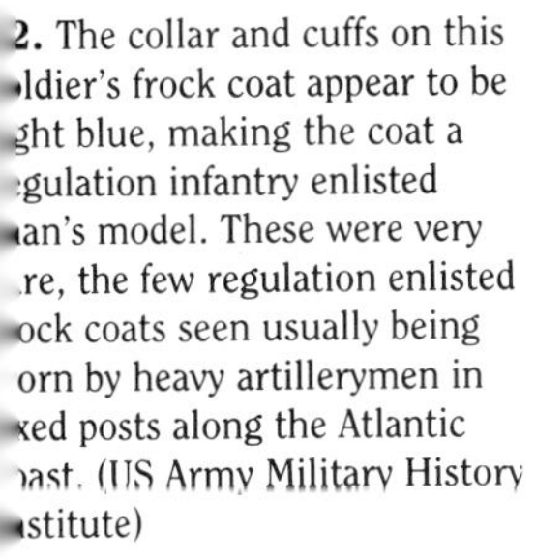

2. The collar and cuffs on this ldier's frock coat appear to be ght blue, making the coat a gulation infantry enlisted an's model. These were very re, the few regulation enlisted ock coats seen usually being orn by heavy artillerymen in xed posts along the Atlantic oast. (US Army Military History stitute)

3. The typical enlisted soldier's othing for most of the war cluded plain grey or brown ousers and matching single-reasted jacket with between ve and nine buttons down the ont. Plain matching epaulettes ere common as well. Buttons ere often of wood rather than gulation brass. (Author's ollection)

4. The plain iron or brass ame buckle, as worn on this infantryman's waist belt, was the most common Confederate Army-issue belt plate. His other equipment includes a percussion cap pouch and plain leather bayonet scabbard. His weapon is an M1842 0.69-calibre smoothbore musket. His frock coat has been trimmed around the collar and down the front, probably in black or red. (Herb Peck Jr collection)

◀45 46▲ 47▼

48▲

5. Private John T. Davis of
labama wears an all grey or
ght brown version of the US
rmy's sack coat and matching
rousers. His weapon is a
ritish-made copy of the Enfield
ifled musket; his bayonet
cabbard, percussion cap pouch
nd cartridge box are on his
aist belt, as was typical of
onfederate infantrymen. (US
rmy Military History Institute)

6. The single-shot smoothbore
istol here is probably a
hotographer's prop. The
ldiers' grey frock coats appear
have black or red collars, the
ldier with the pistol having
lain cuffs and the other one
ith cuffs that match his collar.
heir unit is unknown, but
eir dress is typical of that
orn in 1861–62 by Southern
oops. (Herb Peck Jr collection)

7. Private John Reily, 16th
ississippi Infantry Regiment, wears a plain grey double-breasted frock coat. The 16th was organized in Corinth, Mississippi, in June 1861, and served in the Army of Northern Virginia from the Seven Days' Battle until it was surrendered at Appomattox. At Chancellorsville, 76 per cent of its men were casualties. (John R. Love collection/US Army Military History Institute)

48. The bowie knife with the D-guard was typical of personal weapons carried by Southern troops for several months after joining the army; it was, however, quickly abandoned. The shotgun, too, was probably replaced by a single-shot rifled musket. The drum canteen made of tin, however, was the most common piece of Southern military equipment carried throughout the war. (Herb Peck Jr collection)

49▲

49. Private S. C. Williams served both in Company D, 5th North Carolina State Troops and Company D, 13th North Carolina Light Artillery; it is not known which unit he was in when this photograph was taken. The 5th was organized in July 1861, fighting at the First Manassas and then through Appomattox. The 13th was organized in December 1863, Company D serving with the Army of Tennessee and at the unsuccessful Battle of Bentonville, after which the remainder of that force surrendered. (US Army Military History Institute)

▲50

50. The star on this young soldier's belt plate may stand for Texas, but it might just as well stand for Mississippi, whose troops wore buttons bearing a five-pointed star. The soldier's equipment has been reversed, his cartridge box normally being worn on the rear right hip and the bayonet scabbard on the left. His weapon is an M1855 rifled musket. (Herb Peck Jr collection)

▼51

▲52

51. Private William Ridley enlisted in Petersburg, Virginia, and was killed at Malvern Hill during the Peninsular Campaign. His grey forage cap bears his company letter, F, and his plain grey jacket is made with epaulettes, a common practice. Soldiers in the field almost never wore ties, as he does, and, indeed, white shirts like this were also rare. (US Army Military History Institute)

52. Northern photographers took most of the known pictures of Confederate soldiers – and the soldiers were all too often dead when their photographs were taken. These men were members of Starke's Louisiana Brigade, made up of the 1st, 2nd, 9th, 10th, and 15th Louisiana Infantry Regiments and the 1st Louisiana Battalion, photographed where they fell along the Hagerstown Pike at the Battle of Sharpsburg. Their single-breasted jackets are all plain. (National Archives)

53. Private J. P. Starcher serve in the 3rd Virginia Infantry anc 19th Virginia Cavalry. He coulc have been in either unit when this photograph was taken. Th 3rd came from Portsmouth in July 1861 and served in all the campaigns of the Army of Northern Virginia. The 19th w raised in April 1863, serving in the Shenandoah Valley until disbanded in April 1865. (Tom Williams Collection/US Army Military History Institute)

54. This dummy wears an original Confederate infantryman's uniform and equipment and gives a good id of what the typical infantry private looked like. The unifor is all grey wool, with seven brass buttons down the front, and the weapon is a Richmond made copy of the M1855 rifled musket. The brass belt plate bearing the letters 'CS' was typical of western Confederate rather than of the Army of Northern Virginia. (Smithsonian Institution)

53▼ 54▶

55. Private W. F. Henry, Company G, 6th Tennessee Infantry Regiment, wears the letters 'JG', for Jackson Grays (which became Coy G of the 6th), on the front of his grey forage cap. He is armed with a knife and a Colt revolver, neither of which would last long in actual service. The 6th was in the Army of Tennessee, Henry surrendering with his unit as a sergeant in North Carolina on 1 May 1865. (Herb Peck Jr collection)

56. This man, apparently a member of Ramseur's North Carolina Brigade, was photographed in May 1864 where he fell during the fighting near Spotsylvania, Virginia. The weapon is an Enfield rifled musket; the round tin canteen with rings pressed in its sides was US Army issue. His leather pouch for percussion caps, with a shield front, and his leather cartridge box next to it were worn on his waist belt. (Library of congress)

57. These three men appear to have been stragglers from the Army of Northern Virginia after Gettysburg. The three-day-long battle saw General Lee try to destroy the Army of the Potomac by hitting its right and left flanks and, finally, its centre on 3 July. That final, unsuccessful assault has gone into the history books as Pickett's Charge. (Library of Congress)

56▲ **57▼**

◀55

▲58 ▼59

58. The piping on the coat worn by Private D. R. Cesar, Company E, 1st Local Troops, Georgia Infantry, is odd, to say the least. The waist-level pocket is used to hold the percussion caps, so no separate leather pouch is needed. The unit was raised in Augusta, helping in the unsuccessful defence of the State against Sherman's forces in 1864. (Lee Joyner collection)

59. The weapon lying over the body of this defender of Fort Mahone, who died in April 1865 as the Union troops overran the Southern defence of Petersburg, Virginia, appears to be a US Army M1861 Colt Contract Rifle Musket, one of thousands of captured US Army weapons used by the Confederate Army. The weapon behind him is a US Army smoothbore musket converted from flintlock to percussion cap – and still in service. (Library of Congress)

60. This typical set of Confederate cavalry uniform and equipment, complete with US Army-issue belt plate, is worn by Private J. P. Sellman, Company K, 1st Virginia Cavalry. The unit was formed in July 1861 and was highly feared in the early years of the war. Their charge into the 11th New York at the First Manassas was one of the turning points of that battle. (Charles T. Jacobs collection/US Army Military History Institute)

61. The sabre held by this Virginia cavalryman was made in the Virginia Manufactory in the early 1800s and pressed into service in 1861. His hand gun is a Remington revolver, made in the North, while his all-brass belt plate bears the seal of the State of Virginia. His collar probably has yellow trim with a single button on each side. (Herb Peck Jr collection)

62. Yellow tape is probably used to decorate the collar of the single-breasted jacket worn by Private Bently Weston, 7th South Carolina Cavalry Regiment. The 7th was organized in March 1864 from various understrength units and served in Northern Virginia until surrendered. By 1864, Confederate cavalry was generally outmatched by better-equipped, better-horsed Union cavalry. (Library of Congress)

◀60 61▲ 62▼

◀63 64▲ 65▼

66▲

63. Private J. O. Sheppard, Company F, 6th South Carolina Cavalry, wears a magnificently trimmed copy of the US cavalry jacket, with a US Army-issue belt and sword. He later became the regiment's sergeant major. The 6th, called the Dixie Rangers, was raised in January 1863, serving in South Carolina and then Northern Virginia, and finally surrendering with the Army of Tennessee. (Brig. Gen. James Daniels collection/US Army Military History Institute)

64. Private J. J. Dodd, Company C, 4th South Carolina Cavalry Regiment, holds a copy of the US Army-issue light cavalry sabre. Although issued, this weapon saw little actual use, most cavalry engagements being fought on foot with carbines. The 4th was formed from survivors of the 10th and 12th Cavalry Battalions in January 1863. It served in the deep South until transferred to the Army of Northern Virginia. It later went to the Army of Tennessee, with which it surrendered. (Library of Congress)

65. This well-armed soldier has a Colt revolver on his left and a Starr revolver on his right. Both are tucked into a belt made of painted canvas with a leather strap and brass or iron frame buckle on front. These belts came into being because of leather shortages in the South that forced their use as well as the use of shoes with canvas uppers and wood soles. (Herb Peck Jr collection)

66. These two members of the 6th Virginia Cavalry Regiment are armed with 0.36-calibre Colt 'Navy' revolvers. The man on the left has a percussion cap box on his waist belt, while the other wears a US Army cavalry cap badge. The shirts were often worn instead of jackets in 1861, but these home-made garments failed to last long into the war. The 6th served in the Army of Northern Virginia. (Library of Congress)

▲67

▲68

67. The jacket worn by this man, believed to be a member of the 1st Maryland Cavalry Regiment, is elaborately trimmed. Unfortunately, because of the chemical make-up of photographic film of the 1860s, the exact colours cannot be accurately determined. His checked trousers are certainly civilian, however, and his hat bears a plume, something popular with mounted troops. (Charles T. Jacobs collection/US Army Military History Institute)

68. The jacket and waistcoat worn by Private Francis Jones, 8th Virginia Cavalry Regiment, match in colour and, probably, material. The 8th was formed in early 1862 in western Virginia, serving there and in Tennessee before joining troops in the Shenandoah Valley. It was present at Appomattox but cut its way through Union lines and disbanded after the surrender there. (Library of Congress)

69. This detail of a photograph of a light artillery section abounds in uniform and equipment information. The officer, in the frock coat, carries a cavalry sabre. The man ramming, left, wears a round peaked cap, apparently an M1839 US Army forage cap. The day of muzzle-loading artillery commanding the field, as it had done in Napoleon's time, was past, since rifled muskets could bring down artillery crews before they could do much damage to infantry formations. (Library of Congress)

70. The man ramming on the right-hand gun in the two-gun section wears a red stripe down his leg, while the man standing next to him wears red pointed cuffs and, probably, a standing collar; the others in the section have plain, all-grey jackets. The sergeant, standing next to the young guidon bearer, has an issue light artillery sabre. (Library of Congress)

69▲ 70▼

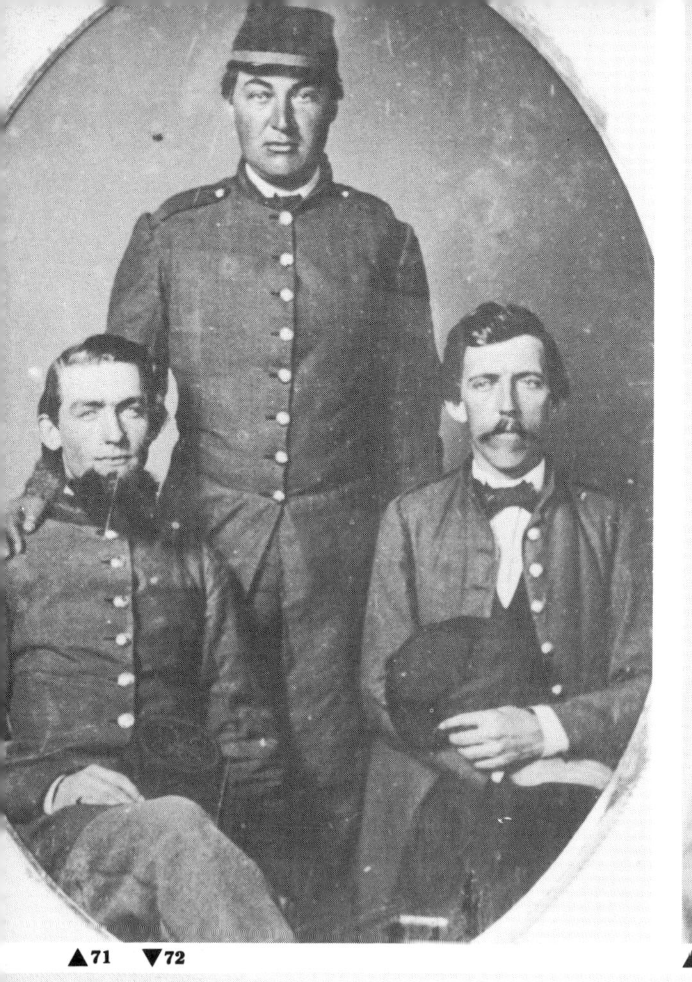

▲71 ▼72

▲73

76▲

71. It is not known what branch of service these men were in, although the dark trim on their coat collars and epaulettes and the dark forage caps with a lighter trefoil design on top suggest the artillery. Despite the uniformity of their coats, all three wear different coloured trousers. The white shirts and ties suggest that the photograph was taken in 1861. (John R. Wernick collection)

72. This motley collection is made up of prisoners from the Army of Tennessee awaiting shipment to a Northern prisoner-of-war camp. Confederate prisoners were not left unhoused and starved, as were Union prisoners, but they still died by the thousands in the cold climates of the camps. In all, 462,634 Confederates became prisoners-of-war, of whom 25,976 died in captivity. (Library of Congress)

73. Virginian Edward Thomas Hoge wears a grey jacket that appears to be made of cotton/wool mixed cloth with a collar of a facing colour, perhaps red for artillery. His buttons appear to be brass but are smaller than usual. A slash pocket over each breast is fastened with a matching brass button. (Hatsy Droke collection/US Army Military History Institute)

74. This soldier, photographed in Nashville, Tennessee, wears the plain jacket typically issued throughout the war. Officially grey, the shades of grey ranged from off-white to almost black. Also worn, at least until 1863, were brown uniforms, ranging from dust coloured to coffee coloured according to locally available dyes. (Author's collection)

75. This man's waistcoat is not only of a lighter colour than his jacket, but also uses small, brass ball buttons instead of the more typical buttons marked with branch-of-service letters or state coats-of-arms. Waistcoats were made at home rather than issued, and hence varied widely. Most, however, came with a small standing collar and three or four patch pockets. (Author's collection)

76. The trim on this Virginia soldier's jacket edges the top and front of his standing collar and then passes down the jacket front. This was a common feature of trimmed jackets or coats. By 1863 most jackets were made without branch-of-service colour trim, despite the fact that such was regulation. (Author's collection)

◀77 78▲ 79▶

77. Commodore French Forrest
vears the uniform of a flag
officer in the Confederate Navy,
vith his cap peak bound in
orass and the gold-embroidered
ouled anchor within a wreath
badge. His sword is a British-
nade regulation Confederate
Navy model, as is his sword belt
plate. Forrest was the head of
the Navy's Bureau of Orders and
Detail. (US Army Military
History Institute)

78. Admiral Franklin Buchanan
commanded the Confederate
Navy's CSS *Virginia* in its
history-making engagement
vith the USS *Monitor* and then
commanded a small squadron in
an unsuccessful attempt to
lefend Mobile Bay against an
overwhelming US Navy
quadron that included a
number of *Monitor*-Class ships.
His uniform is essentially the
ame as Forrest's, with an
xecutive loop on the top gold-
ace stripe on his cuffs.
Buchanan's uniform now in the
Maryland Historical Society
collection, however, bears
Maryland State buttons. (US
Army Military History Institute)

79. Midshipman John Morris
Morgan's rank is indicated by
the three medium-sized buttons
worn on each cuff combined
with his lack of shoulder straps.
A passed midshipman would
wear a gold stripe on each
shoulder. Morgan, however,
wears the same British-made
sword as Commodore French
Forrest. Moreover, he buttons
his coat at the collar in
accordance with regulations.
(US Army Military History
Institute)

80

81▲

82▲ 83▼

·. Although there are no
ıown published Marine Corps
ess regulations, it appears
at most officers wore Army-
·le uniforms with dark blue as
·ranch-of-service colour. First
ꞔutenant D. G. Raney of the
·rps also wears Russian
oulder knots, regulation in
ꞔ US Marine Corps and
mmon among Confederate
ırine officers. HIs belt plate is
JS Army officer's model.
ney was a Marine officer on
CSS *Tennessee* in the
gagement at Mobile Bay.

. First Lieutenant Frances H.
meron spent most of his time
the Marine Corps on staff
ty, although his first duty was
h the Corps' Company A. His
lar is folded down, so it
ınot be told if he wears Army-
le insignia on it, but the gold
strian knot is regulation for
rank. His coat appears to be
unusually dark grey.
ıtional Archives)

82. There are no known photographs of enlisted Marines; they appear to have worn grey frock coats with black trim on the collar and cuffs and a single row of seven buttons, along with plain dark blue caps. This man's uniform may be that of the Corps, with dark-colour piping around the collar and down the coat front as well as on the cuff edges. (US Army Military History Institute)

83. Marines in the Richmond area, part of the force defending against the 1864 assault towards the city from the Bermuda Hundred, were described as wearing jackets like those worn in the Army. This corporal's dark cap and chevrons (worn pointing up rather than down) suggests the possibility that he is an enlisted Marine. Revolvers were often issued for shipboard use, being easier to wield in confined areas than muskets. (George M. Cress collection)